Golden Rules of Writing

Sheikh Muhammad Ibraheem

INTRODUCTION

I always wanted to do something that changes the perception of people on this planet, so I choose to write books on various topics. Mostly I write related to my engineering research field, but I also love to write various stories.

Becoming a writer or anything else does not require you to learn and read a lot. It requires your focus and passion. If you are passionate about something then you will work 24 hours straight. If your passion is writing then you will write no matter how bad your writing is, you just write.

This is how I started writing, I knew that books are the only medium of keeping records, history, and knowledge. So I choose this medium over any other.

I started writing a couple of years ago. At that moment I accidentally wrote 50 pages without knowing. After reading my own 50-page research draft and correcting mistakes. I quickly came to know that I can excel in it. If I just focus.

This book will tell you how to become an author, especially a self-published author. How to select a niche and how to market your book. All you need is an ISBN number, a laptop, and some nice thoughts.

ABOUT BOOK

This book is written to provide you with all the necessary knowledge in order to become an author. The book will guide you on how to bring thoughts in your mind, how to shape them in a story, how to write with the fear of grammatical errors, and how to overcome those fear.

The central motive of this book is to develop the love of reading, writing, and delivering knowledge through the medium of pages.

ABOUT AUTHOR

Sheikh Muhammad Ibraheem (Born November 20, 2000) is a Pakistani Author and Electrical Engineer. He will receive his BS in Electrical Engineering from The University of Lahore (2023-InshaAllah). He has also received many certificates in Astrophysics, Particle Physics, Electric Power System etc from some of the most reputed universities across the world including the Australian National University, Open University UK, The State University of New York, The University of Edinburgh, etc. Since 2022, he is writing technical articles for "The Engineering Post" which is a national engineering magazine. Since 2021 Ibraheem has self-published many short and long books on engineering and technology. Ibraheem is enthusiastic about modern world technology and currently researching in clean and renewable energy sources, microgrids etc.

Ibraheem provides various publication, web development, and other services for the young authors, entrepreneurs. For more information on Ibraheem books and services please visit (https://sheikhibraheem.com)

Table of Contents

Golden Rules of Writing

How to Become a Self-Published Author

Contents

Rule # One

WHY THE BOOKS?

I f you want to become an author. The first thing you need to understand is the word *"book"* according to Wikipedia, "The book is the medium of recording knowledge in the form of writing or images."

Writing anything is very old. It dates back to thousands of years, yet it is a perfect way of keeping a record.

We think that a book is just a group of hundreds or thousands of pages binded together. We think that every page of a book has just these weird symbols that we call alphabets. Connecting these symbols in a specific order gives us a word. A word that describes a lot of things. A word that has meaning. A word that contains a fraction of knowledge.

These books have proved to be the guiding light in the darkest hours of any human being. With this new technology of the 21st century, people are losing interest in books, they are moving towards audiobooks, podcasts, and whatever. The real joy is in reading a book.

Let me explain to you, in a nutshell, the importance of books and reading in our lives.
If you want to be a good writer, be a good reader.
If you want to be successful, be a good reader.
If you seek knowledge, be a good reader.
If you want to enjoy, be a good reader.

But just don't go, grab a book and start reading it without a purpose. Reading without a purpose will do you no good. It will only result in a waste of time.

Before reading any book, paper or article. Think about the anatomy of the book. If you mastered it, you have mastered everything.

Rule # Two

BE A GOOD READER

You now want to read a book, but why do you want to read it? Is it because you have just read the first chapter of this book or you are passionate about reading anything?

If you want to be a good reader then you need to understand the books, papers, and articles. Every book, paper, or article tells the story in its own way. Let me make it much clearer for you to understand.

Imagine you want to buy a car. You go to a car showroom and the showroom owner shows you a different car. You buy a car and then drive it home. But wait this is not how it works right? You ask the owner or car specialist about the details of the car, for example, its manufacturer, its model, its top speed, etc. You are asking because you know what every car has in common, you know about its basic functions, how to drive it, you know which manufacturer is the best, and most importantly which is best for you. You provide all these details and buy your dream car.

Similarly, the books are the same, there is a vast variety of books just like cars, and there are thousands of publishers and authors just like manufacturers, and there are some basic rules of reading just like basic car functions.

Let's observe what every book has in common. In every book, you will find the following from the first page to the last page.
1. Book Title & Subtitle.
2. Copyright Notice.
3. Publisher and Author Biography.
4. Dedications and Acknowledgements.
5. Book Introduction.
6. Table of Contents.
7. Chapters.
8. Summary.
9. The End.

Every book, whether its fiction, non-fiction, textbooks etc., all have the above things in different orders.

I've observed people quickly jump to the topic that they want to read or benefit from and then are confused about what they are reading. Mostly when people are reading a textbook for example an engineering book they just skim it. Most people quit a novel after reading the first few chapters of it.

The question is why people are so confused while reading or are bored of reading it. The real answer is they don't even know what they are looking for exactly. There is a reason why every book has an introduction, an ending, a table of contents, and an author introduction.

The introduction of any book provides a reader about what he is about to read in the following chapters, what will he learn after reading it, or how will he read it.

The author's biography helps him understand what kind of person the author was and why did he write the book.

The table of contents helps in understanding which chapter should be read first and why should it be.

So next time when you open a book thoroughly read it's introduction, table of contents, author section, and about sections. These pages will help you in understanding the overall motive of the book.

If you want to skim then skim the list of contents. This will help in finding you right topic and you will also be aware of what to read and how to read it.

Rule # Three

WHY BECOME A WRITER?

You now want to write a book, but why do you want to write it? Are writing because it's your passion or just because you have read many books and now want to earn fame and money?

It doesn't matter what is your matter behind the writing, what does matter is what will you write. If writing is so simple then why not everyone is a writer? Writing on a piece of paper is just like art on canvas. Both author and artist have to do years of practice, and have to face failure as well. Both artists and authors depict their thoughts on canvas and paper respectively, the only difference is that one is using paint and brushers for it while the other is using pen and paper for it.

If you want to become a writer then you really need to do the following.

1. Generate an Idea.
2. Work on that Idea.
3. Write Fearlessly.
4. Re-write and Improve Grammar.
5. Publish the Idea.

This is the simplest way of writing any book. But in this book, we are motivated to self-publish a book. This is how we are going to do it.

1. Generation of Thoughts.
2. Writing those Thoughts.
3. Book Formatting.
4. Mode of Publications.
5. How to Self-Publish.
6. International Distributions.
7. International Bank Accounts.
8.

Rule # Four

YOUR THOUGHTS & NICHES

Now, you are interested in writing a book, but the biggest problem you are facing right now is where to begin with.

Before you begin writing anything, you first need to focus on what kind of ideas and thoughts your mind creates. If you are a literature student or a professional then writing fiction novels, stories, and fantasies will be an excellent choice for you. But if you are from a professional background e.g. engineering and medicine then writing a research book will be a lot easier for you to begin with.

If you are not familiar with the niches and are often confused which niche you should choose as your career, then allow me to explain it I depth for you.

Genre Fiction which is also known as popular fiction niche used for fictional written work. Most of the fiction like fantasies, crime, science fiction, novels, and romances are written in this genre.

Any text or piece of media that makes an honest effort to present facts about the real world rather than being based on fantasy is considered non-fiction. The goal of non-fiction is often to convey subjects in an objective manner using historical, scientific, and empirical data. Non-fiction does, however, sometimes veer into the more personal ground, including truly held opinions on current events.

Fiction and Non-Fiction are the two main genres in which one can write a book. Most textbooks, biographies, and histories are non-fiction whereas novels, stories, and fantasies are fiction books.

Rule # Five

YOUR FIRST FICTION PARAGRAPH

Writing the first paragraph or chapter is usually the most difficult one, especially in the fiction genre. So when you have decided that you want to be a writer and want to be a best-seller then you need to focus on the following things.

1. Story that captures the mind of readers.
2. Competition in your genre.
3. Competition in the Language of writing.
4. Your promotion strategies.

The first one which is to capture the mind of readers is the most difficult among all.

If you have mastered in capturing the mind of readers through your words and stories then it is just a matter of time that you will become a successful writer.

Let me tell you how I capture the mind of my readers. I don't start writing the book and think about what next should I add in the paragraph to make it more capturing.

I usually spent a couple of months in finding a perfect story that captures the reader's mind. I work on the thoughts and ideas for a few months.

What I do is that I think about the topic of the story and make a complete draft in my mind and then I write it down. This gives me leverage on both time and thoughts.

Divide your book into ten different chapters. Keep the chapters to a maximum of 5 pages and starts writing. Once your ten chapters are completed then re-edit all of them if necessary.

Keep the book length according to the story that you want to tell. Don't go for 200 or 300 pages just to extend the page count. If your story has 100 pages and is worth reading people will read and buy it. If your story has 300 pages and it's not good enough people will not buy it at all.

So when you are writing the first chapter or paragraph of your book write something that captures the mind of the reader and forces him to read the next chapters of your book.

If you are writing a crime or horror book then start with the suspense and keep it for the rest of your book. Break that suspense in the perfect area of your story that surprises the reader with joy.

If you are writing a textbook then start with some facts that are not available in any other book in your genre. Or explains something new in your book.

Every book that you write must have new thoughts, new ways of doing some things, and new techniques. People always move towards new and novel things.

In the market, people are always looking for some kind of twist and novelty.

Rule # Six

SELF PUBLICATION OR TRADITIONAL PUBLICATION

Rejection is the one thing that people are so afraid of. People are afraid of failure and hesitate to take the first step. Most people don't even start writing because they believe that the publisher will turn down his book and their amazing story will not be published.

It is true that traditional publishers turn down author books or charge thousands of dollars to publish them. Fear of rejection and expense on the book is what de-motivates people in quit writing.

In the 21st century we are living in the global village. Almost every country is now connected on the internet. The biggest used language is English.

In the first chapter, I explained that people are not interested in reading paperback books. They are usually interested in reading eBooks and audiobooks. So if paperback and bulk printing is expensive for you then go for eBooks and audiobooks.

In order to publish your book you first need to understand what is traditional publication and self-publication.

The procedure of publishing a book, manuscript, or other written work through a traditional publisher is known as traditional publishing. An organization that focuses on the purchase, editing, production, and dissemination of written works is known as a conventional publisher. Usually, the publisher will make an investment in the work by editing, formatting, and marketing it, and the author will get a cut of the profits.

Authors submit their writing to publishers and literary agencies, who then decide whether to accept it for publication, according to the traditional publishing model. When a publisher decides to publish a piece, they usually provide the author an advance against future revenues and make investments on the editing, formatting, and marketing of the piece. The book will then be distributed by the publisher to bookstores and internet sellers.

Traditional publishing might be an excellent choice for authors who want the assistance and tools of a publisher, such as editing, formatting, and marketing, but the process can be drawn out, and more difficult to persuade a traditional publisher to accept work, and the royalties might be smaller.

In this book, we are interested in self-publication. So it is important for us to understand what is self-publication.

Self-publication is the act of publishing a book, manuscript, or other written work on one's own without the assistance of a traditional publisher. As an alternative, it is the author's duty to edit, format, and publish the work, typically doing so using online distribution platforms like Barnes & Noble Press or Amazon Kindle Direct Publishing. If an author is unsuccessful in finding a traditional publisher, self-publishing could be a fantastic alternative. who aspire to more autonomy in the publication and dissemination of their work. However, self-published works might not receive the same editorial and marketing support as officially published works, and consumers and industry experts might have different perspectives on them.

Rule # Seven

HOW TO DO SELF-PUBLICATION?

Now, we want to self-publish our great story. But how can I publish it? How should I distribute it? How can I reach the readers without any experience?

These are the questions that come in the mind of writer, when he is about to self-publish his first book. In order to become a successful self-published author, you need to have the following.

1. Self – Publication Platforms.
2. Author Social Media Platforms.
3. Author Website (not necessary).
4. Distribution Platforms.

If any author is successful in these above four things then he will become a successful author in only a few years.

Self-Publication Platform:

The first thing is an author need is a self-publication platform. Trough which he can read its reader. Note that for self-publication you need two things.

1. ISBN number.
2. Copyright Notice. (if it is protected / non-public domain work.)

If an author has an ISBN number and has a copyright notice then he can self-publish anywhere he likes to. As he owns all the rights to his book.

There are hundreds of different self-publication platforms that are totally free to publish.

1. Amazon Kindle Direct Publication.
2. Apple Books.
3. Google Play Books.
4. Barnes & Nobel Press.
5. Street Lib.
6. Gum road.

Amazon, Apple, Google, Barnes & Nobel and streetlib provides free ISBN to its authors and publish the book within 72 hours. They only take their commission and publish your book for free on their platform. In this book we are going to discuss the Amazon Kindle and Google Play Books.

The paid self-publication platforms include.
1. Ingram spark.
2. Lulu.
3. Smash words.
4. Publish Drive.
5. XinXii
6. Reedsy.

These just a few out of hundreds of paid self-publication platforms.

Author Social Media Platforms.
Author social media platforms are important for the author to connect to its readers. The most used author social media platforms include.
1. Goodreads.
2. Story Graph.
3. Twitter.
4. Instagram.
5. Facebook.

An author must have a professional page or account on all of these platforms in order to attract readers and connect with them. A strong connection with the reader develops some sincere relations between authors and readers.

Author Website (not necessary).

An author must have its own official website like I have (https://sheikhibraheem.com). The website of any author or professional is an excellent way of searching and connection. If an author has its own website people can buy books, easily connect on social media platforms, etc.

Distribution Platforms.

Now just self-publications, author social media platforms, and a website is not enough to become a best seller. The more your book is searched on the internet the more likely is that people will buy your book.

For example, you are an American author and people in Pakistan want to buy your book. They have seen it on social media but can not buy it. How can you provide your book to them? The distribution platforms solve this problem.

There are hundreds of distribution platforms mostly self-publications platforms are the distribution platforms. But the one I like mostly are.

1. Streetlib.
2. Draft to Digital
3. Ingram Spark.

Let's start with the self publication on Amazon Kindle Now.

Rule # Eight

AMAZON KINDLE DIRECT PUBLICATIONS

I n this chapter, we are going to learn about self-publishing with Amazon KDP. Before doing that let's learn about what Amazon KDP is?

Authors and publishers can publish a range of materials through Amazon KDP (Kindle Direct Publishing), including eBooks, paperbacks, and audiobooks. The material may fall under a number of genres, including poetry, academic writing, fiction, and non-fiction. However, there are some content requirements set down by KDP that must be followed, such as those governing objectionable or illegal content, plagiarism, and intellectual property rights. Before posting on the platform, authors should carefully read and abide by these rules.

KDP was launched in November 2007, by Amazon. Since then it has become the world's largest eBook store and self-publication platform.

eBook Publication:

On KDP an author can publish his eBook easily. KDP take up to 72 hours of review once the book is submitted on their platform. In order to publish an eBook on KDP ISBN is not necessary. Amazon KDP provides its own book number called ASIN number also known as Amazon Standard Identification Number.

Amazon KDP accepts Docx, Doc, PDF, Mobi, and ePub for publishing. Amazon KDP is best in this regard as it accepts more than one format for eBook publication. Most other self-publication platforms accept only ePub and Mobi.

Up to 70% royalty is offered on the KDP eBook platform.

Hardcover & Paperback Publication:

Amazon also provides paperback and hardcover facilities to the authors. Authors can easily publish their books in paperback and hardcover.

Amazon has made this possible through POD "print on demand". POD is a feature through which a reader can buy a book and the book will be printed on his demand and will be shipped to his address. All of this is completely done by the Amazon KDP itself.

Up to 60% royalty is offered to the author in paperback and hardcover format.

Overall Amazon KDP is an excellent platform to publish books and get revenue from it.

In the next chapters we will learn how to create an account on Amazon KDP and publish first book.

Rule # Nine

ACCOUNT CREATION ON KDP

Now, we want to create an account on Amazon KDP. To create an account on Amazon KDP we need a few things.

1. Email account.
2. Phone Number.
3. Tax Information.
4. Name.
5. Address.
6. Username.
7. Payment Methods.

In order to create an account you need to signup using your email and password. You will also need to add your phone number for extra security.

Once your account is created you need to fulfill these three things.

1. My profile.

2. Payment method,
3. Tax information.

After fulfilling the three sections, your account will be legally ready to publish any kind of book. Let's start with the first section now.

My Profile:

My profile is the basic section that contains all of your details like name, date of birth identity number etc. In this section you need to provide the following information.

1. Legal Name (Name written of Passport or ID Card).
2. Date of Birth (Must be at least 18 years old.)
3. Country of Residence.
4. Address.
5. City.
6. State / Province.
7. Postal Code.
8. Phone Number.
9. Business Type (Individual or Cooperate)

The individual business is a business in which an author is the owner of all the books that will be published by the author or the publisher. Cooperate business is one in which more than one person is involved and the revenue is shared among them.

Keep is mind that select this carefully as Tax information and payment methods depend on it. I will recommend that one should choose the individual business as an author.

Payment Methods:

For getting paid on Amazon you will need to provide your payment method. In this section, you need the following things.

1. Bank Name.
2. Bank Country.
3. Account Holder Name.
4. Account Number

This is the standard requirement that is needed by any country. I recommend United States Account. For that you will need.

1. Bank Country (United States of America)
2. Account Name.
3. Account Number.
4. Account Type (Checking or Savings.)
5. Routing Number

If you are an American citizen you can easily get these account details. However, if you are not an American citizen all of these details can be easily provided to you by Payoneer. This book will also guide you on creating a successful Payoneer account.

Tax Information:

The final step of account creation on KDP is to provide Tax information. In this section you need to provide the following information.

1. Business Type (Individual or Cooperate.)
2. US citizen claim or foreign person.
3. Working on someone's behalf or you are the sole owner.
4. Legal Name.
5. Country of Residence.
6. Permanent and Mailing Address.
7. TIN number.

If you are non-US person then you have to submit a US W-8 form.

Rule # Ten

INTERNATIONAL PAYMENT METHODS

We, know that in order to receive payments from the internet, we need a payment method or an international US dollar, Euro, or UK pound bank account. But getting this from individual countries and continents can be very problematic. A US company called Payoneer solves this problem.

Online payment solutions and international money transfer services are offered by Payoneer, a reputable provider of financial services. Since its establishment in 2005, the company has grown to be a well-liked choice for companies, independent contractors, and people who need a safe and dependable platform for sending and receiving payments internationally.

Payoneer' s ability to enable cross-border payments in more than 150 currencies is one of its important benefits since it enables customers to send and receive money in their own currencies without the need for pricy currency conversions. This makes it the perfect platform for cross-border transactions, especially for independent contractors and small enterprises that interact with clients from other nations.

Additionally, Payoneer provides a selection of payment options, such as virtual accounts, mass payouts, and international payment processing, to meet the unique requirements of various users. These services are made to aid companies in streamlining their payment procedures, lowering transaction costs, and boosting productivity.

Payoneer provides a variety of financial services in addition to its payment solutions, including as prepaid debit cards, currency exchange, and working capital loans. These services are intended to give consumers more financial freedom and support, assisting them in developing and growing their enterprises.

Utilizing Payoneer's user-friendly platform and customer assistance is another important perk. The platform's user-friendly features and straightforward interfaces make it simple to manage payments and keep track of transactions. Additionally, the business offers users round-the-clock customer service to help with any queries or problems they may have.

In conclusion, Payoneer is a well-known financial services provider of online payment options and international money transfer services. It is the perfect platform for companies, independent contractors, and individuals who need a secure and dependable platform for sending and receiving payments internationally because it can facilitate cross-border payments in more than 150 currencies and offers a variety of payment solutions and financial products. Customers of all experience levels favor it because of its user-friendly platform and customer service.

You must register for a Payoneer account and go through the verification process in order to receive a Payoneer bank account. The steps are as follows:

1. Create a Payoneer account: Click the "Sign Up" button on the Payoneer website. Set a password and enter your contact and personal information.

2. Verify your account: After you register for a Payoneer account, you will be prompted to prove your identity. This is accomplished by uploading a piece of official identification, like a passport or driver's license, and giving some other details.

3. After your account has been validated, you can select the payout method of your choice. Depending on where you are, Payoneer offers a variety of payout options, such as bank transfer, prepaid Mastercard, and regional e-wallets.

4. Open a bank account: If you decide to use a bank transfer, you can open a Payoneer virtual bank account to accept payments from businesses and customers who need a bank account to do so. Go to the "Receive" page in your Payoneer account and select the "Global Payment Service" option to register for a virtual bank account. You'll be asked to choose your preferred currency and to supply some further information.

5. Receive payments: As soon as your virtual bank account is approved, you can begin getting paid by businesses and customers who need a bank account to make a payment. The money will be transferred to your virtual bank

account through Payoneer, from which you can withdraw it to a real bank account or spend it for online purchases.

Overall, opening a Payoneer bank account is a simple and uncomplicated process that enables you to accept payments from businesses and clients all around the world.

Rule # Eleven

COPYRIGHT AND ISBNS

Publication on Amazon KDP is extremely easy. But most authors need ISBNs and copyright notices. It is legal to use the Amazon ISBN but Amazon doesn't allow the use of its ISBN on any other platform.

Moreover, the copyright of any content or book can be easily done through creative commons. In this chapter, we will focus on copyright and ISBNs for any book. First Let's start with the ISBNs.

As an author If you want an ISBN you can easily purchase an ISBN from ISBN's official website, the national library (if they provide one) or any other website that provides ISBNs. While purchasing ISBNs bulk purchase costs less compare to any single purchase.

ISBN is only issued once. This means that once an ISBN is issued to a book it can never be transferred to any other book and can also be never used for more than one book.

For example, the eBook "Golden Rules of Writing" has an issued ISBN. This ISBN can never be used for any other book and can also not be used for paperback, hardcover, or audiobook. If my book is published in eBook, paperback, and audiobook format then there must be three different ISBNs. And the author has to purchase three ISBNs

Copyright is a crucial legal idea that is important for safeguarding the creative works of people and organizations. This protection promotes innovation and creativity across a range of industries and enables creators to profit from their original works.

For a specific amount of time, copyright law gives artists the sole authority to manage the use, distribution, and reproduction of their works. The nature of work and the nation in which it was produced affect how long a copyright is valid. The copyright period typically extends for the creator's lifetime plus a certain number of years after their passing.

Copyright protection has several advantages. It gives artists the power to decide how their work is used and distributed, opening the door to financial benefits and chances for further innovation. Additionally, copyright protection promotes the production of new works by providing an incentive for authors to devote time, energy, and money to refining their concepts.

In conclusion, copyright protection is crucial for authors because it gives them the unique rights to manage how their works are used and distributed, ensuring that they maintain ownership and control over their works. In order to preserve your rights and make sure that your works are being used legally, it is crucial for authors to mark their creations with a copyright notice, register their copyright, and seek legal counsel.

Creative Commons:

A nonprofit organization called Creative Commons offers free, standardized licenses for creative works that enable authors to share their creations with others while still having some control over how those works are utilized. Since its establishment in 2001, the company has grown to be a well-liked choice for artists who want to share their works online without giving up ownership or control of their works.

Depending on their interests and requirements, authors can pick from a variety of Creative Commons licenses. These licenses enable authors to designate the circumstances under which their works may be accessed and used by others, as well as how they may be shared, updated, and distributed.

The ability to authorize or prohibit commercial usage, specify whether modifications are permitted, and demand attribution or credit to the original creator are only a few of the essential characteristics of Creative Commons licenses. Depending on their tastes and requirements, creators can select one of six basic licenses, ranging from the most liberal (CC0) to the most rigid (CC BY-NC-ND).

Creators can get a number of advantages by using Creative Commons licenses, such as more visibility and publicity for their creations, access to a larger audience, and the capacity to cooperate and share knowledge with others. It also provides an alternative to conventional copyright law, which many creators find to be convoluted and challenging to understand. In addition to music, art, literature, and software, Creative Commons has grown to be a popular choice for artists across a variety of industries. To enable people to share and use their contributions, many online services, including Wikipedia, Flickr, and SoundCloud, adopt Creative Commons licensing.

In conclusion, Creative Commons offers free, uniform licenses for artistic creations that let authors share their works with others while yet having some control over how those works are utilized. Creators can gain access to a wider audience and gain more recognition and publicity for their creations by using Creative Commons licenses, among other advantages. Additionally, it provides an alternative to conventional copyright legislation, facilitating creators' sharing and teamwork while maintaining ownership and control over their works.

Rule # Twelve

APPEALING BOOK COVERS

There is a very famous quotation, *"Don't judge a book by its cover."* This is true one must never judge a book by its cover this is because every book contains some valuable information and knowledge. But we can also not neglect that people do judge a book by its cover.

According to a survey people buy those books that are appealing to them by their front book cover. In self-publication or any traditional publication. The book cover really matters.

If the book cover is eye- captivating and worth reading then people are more likely to read the introduction of your book and are more likely to buy them.

If your content is great but the book cover is not much appealing then only a handful of people are going to look at it and buy it.

So, it is important to create a perfect book cover for your book. There are hundreds of free software and website that can help you in designing the perfect book covers for your book. The most reputable in this case is Canva.

Canva is a well-known online graphic design tool that enables users to produce all kinds of visual content, such as book covers, presentations, flyers, posters, social media graphics, and more. It has an intuitive user interface with drag-and-drop capabilities, templates that can be customized, and a vast library of design components, such as fonts, photos, and graphics.

Canva is a great tool for both experts and amateurs because it gives users the freedom to create designs from scratch or edit pre-existing templates to suit their preferences. Its vast template library includes designs for a variety of creative fields, including marketing, advertising, education, and personal branding.

Additionally, Canva provides team members with collaboration capabilities so they can work on the same project together, exchange feedback, and make changes in real time. It is a great option for small teams or distant workers that need to collaborate on projects because of this.

Along with a paid edition that gives access to additional design components, features, and functionality, Canva also offers a free version with fewer capabilities. Greater flexibility and design possibilities are available in the premium edition, which is available via subscription.

Overall, Canva is a flexible and user-friendly tool that offers a great way to create graphic content for both personal and business purposes. Anyone who wants to create attractive, high-quality designs fast and effortlessly will find it to be the best option because of its user-friendly interface, extensive library of templates, and design elements.

Rule # Thirteen

PUBLISHING YOUR BOOK ON KINDLE

S O, far we have written our book, created an account on Amazon KDP, and obtained ISBNs and copyright notice for our book. We have created a stunning book cover. Now we are only a step away from publishing our book worldwide.

Publishing your eBook on Kindle is a piece of cake. As now we have all things, we need to publish. Let's start publication. The following steps will help you publish your first eBook on Kindle same steps will be followed for publishing paperback and hardcover on Kindle.

1. Open your KDP after signing in into your account.

2. In the dashboard find the big yellow button "create."

3. Click the "create" button and select which format you want to publish, eBook, paperback, or hardcover.

4. Click "create eBook" and start filling in all the required details.

5. Once all the details are complete click the submit button for the review. You will receive an email regarding the review of your book.

Kindle eBook Details:

In this section, author has to provide all the necessary details of his book. Following is the list of details that are asked by the KDP.

1. Language of the eBook.

2. eBook Title and Subtitle.

3. eBook Series (if your eBook is a part of any series.)

4. Edition Number (optional.)

5. Author Name.

6. Contributors and Co-Author Names (if any.)

7. eBook Description (Usually write a compelling and clear description that helps a reader why he should purchase this book.)

8. Publishing Rights.

9. Keywords (up to 7, keywords help in searching your book on Amazon and on Google. Carefully choose your keywords as they may increase or decrease your sales.)
10. eBook Category (Select any 2 categories that are best for your book.)
11. Select the Age or Grade for kids and the type of your audience (optional.)
12. Pre-Order your eBook (if you want your eBook then select a pre-order date and continue.)

Kindle eBook Contents:

In this section, an author has to provide the manuscript, ISBN, and book cover. Following is the list of things that are asked by the KDP.

1. Manuscript Submission. (Author must upload KPF, ePub, or docx file of his book here. If the book is in pre-order, then he can submit it a few days before the release of the book.)
2. Kindle eBook cover (Here the author can upload the eBook cover that he has created in canva or can create a cover here as well.)
3. Kindle eBook ISBN (Here the author can provide an ISBN of his book and his publisher if he has any. Note that kindle assigns ISBNs to

paperback and hardcover. It automatically assigns ASINs to the eBooks.)

4. Kindle eBook Review (Once all the content is uploaded a review will be generated to check how the book will appear to the reader. If there are any errors the author has to fix them. In order to move forward. If the review is passed only then author can move towards the final step.)

Kindle eBook Pricing and Distribution:

In this section, an author has to decide the pricing of his book. He also has to select in which countries he wants to sell his book or how he wants his book to be distributed by Amazon.

1. Kindle Select Enrollment (Optional, It is to maximize the royalties.)
2. Territories (In how many countries author wants his book to be available? If all are selected then the book will be available. However, if the individual is selected then an author can select from 245 different territories.)
3. Primary Market Place (Better to select Amazon.com)
4. Pricing and Royalty (Here an author can price his book. If 70% royalty is selected then his

book minimum price must be at least $2.99 and if 35% royalty is selected then his book must be at least $0.99)

5. Terms and Conditions (This is the last step, By agreeing to the terms and conditions of Amazon KDP, an author can submit his book for review. It will take up to 72 hours for to approve.)

Paperback and Hardcover Submission

Paperback and hardcover will have the same procedure for uploading the book. Here an author can submit the PDF version of his book. This is a plus point in Amazon KDP as most other platforms require ePub or Mobi files for paperback and hardcover.

Rule # Fourteen

AMAZON KINDLE CREATE SOFTWARE

Kindle create is software provided by Amazon KDP to create ePub or Mobi files that are best for the Kindle platform. In Kindle Create author can create the **KPF** files of his books. Here an author can create reflowable, print replica and comics. Let's learn in-depth about this software.

Kindle Create is a robust desktop publishing software developed by Amazon to assist authors and publishers in simply creating and formatting their books for publication on the Kindle platform. The software is intended to simplify the process of publishing an eBook for Kindle, allowing users to focus on writing and editing their content while Kindle Create handles formatting and layout.

Kindle Create's ability to import manuscripts from a variety of file formats, including Microsoft Word, HTML, and PDF, is one of its primary advantages. This allows authors to easily turn their existing works into Kindle-ready eBooks without requiring considerable formatting effort. Kindle Create also provides users with a variety of book templates to pick from, which may be adjusted to meet specific needs. The pre-designed templates can save time and effort in the self-publishing process, which is especially beneficial for authors who do not have a background in graphic design or desktop publishing.

Kindle Create also has a variety of interactive features, such as photographs, tables, and lists, that may be added to an eBook. These elements can assist to break up long blocks of text, make the eBook more visually appealing, and provide readers with more information and context. Authors can also use Kindle Create to create a table of contents and chapter headings, which will automatically update when the book is updated or revised.

Another important feature of Kindle Create is the opportunity to preview the eBook across many devices. This enables authors and publishers to preview their book on several Kindle devices, such as the Kindle Paperwhite and Kindle Fire. Users may confirm that the final result looks as expected and that there are no formatting or layout errors that may influence the readability of the book by previewing the eBook on several devices.

Overall, Kindle Create is a fantastic tool for authors and publishers looking to self-publish on the Kindle platform. Its user-friendly interface and pre-designed templates make it simple to generate professional-looking eBooks, while its range of interactive elements and previewing options assist to guarantee that the final output is visually appealing as well as practical. Kindle Create is a vital tool for anyone who wishes to publish their work on Kindle, whether you are a seasoned author or just starting out.

Rule # Fifteen

GOOGLE PLAY BOOKS PARTNER CENTER

Google is the largest search engine on the planet. Every day billions of people use Google to surf the internet. Google Play Books is a Google-developed online eBook and audiobook platform that provides readers with access to a diverse assortment of digital books and audiobooks for purchase or rent. It has a wide assortment of genres, including fiction, nonfiction, textbooks, and children's books. Readers can read their purchased or leased books from any internet-connected device, including phones, tablets, and laptops.

One of the primary advantages of Google Play Books is its cross-platform interoperability. Users can access their books from any world wide web device and seamlessly switch between devices while reading.

This is especially useful for readers who want to read on their phones during their daily commute but prefer to use their tablet or computer at home.

Google Play Books, in addition to a large selection of books, provides a number of features to enhance the reading experience. The reader can, for example, change the font size, background color, and line spacing to make the content easier to read. They can also annotate the book with notes, highlights, and bookmarks, making it easy to return to favorite portions or vital information. Readers may also use the platform's built-in dictionary to seek up unknown words as they read.

Google Play Books, in addition to a large selection of books, provides a number of features to enhance the reading experience. Readers can change the font size, background color, and line spacing, for example, to make the information easier to read. They can also annotate the text with notes, highlights, and bookmarks, allowing them to quickly return to favorite portions or key material. Readers can also use the platform's built-in dictionary to seek up unknown words as they read.

With so many benefits on Google Play Books. The real question is how to publish on Google Play Books. Google has launched a platform called Google Play Books Partner Center through which authors and publishers can easily publish their books.

Google Play Books Partner Center is a Google platform that permits publishers and self-published authors to publish and sell eBooks on Google Play Books. To assist publishers and authors in creating and distributing their eBooks, the platform provides uploading and formatting tools, sales and performance reports, and marketing and promotional tools.

One of Google Play Books Partner Center's primary benefits is its ability to make self-publishing straightforward and accessible. Users may upload eBooks in a variety of file formats, including EPUB and PDF, and employ the platform's formatting capabilities to verify their eBook appears professional and operates properly throughout a variety of devices. The platform also provides a variety of templates and directions to assist users in creating eBooks that fit the requirements for publication on the Google Play Books store.

Google Play Books Partner Center also offers a variety of marketing and promotional tools, such as the ability to generate discount codes and provide free eBook previews. This can assist publishers and authors in reaching new audiences and increasing sales. The platform also provides customers with access to a variety of marketing resources and best practices, allowing them to get the most out of their promotional efforts.

Google Play Books Partner Center also offers a wide range of advertising and promotional tools, such as the ability to generate coupon codes and provide free eBook previews. This can help publishers and authors reach new audiences and increase revenues. The platform also gives customers access to a variety of marketing resources and best practices, helping them to make the most of their promotional efforts.

The biggest disadvantage of Google Play Books Partner Center is that it is only available in few countries. Google Play Books Partner Center is available in numerous countries worldwide. The platform was available in over 70 countries as of my knowledge cutoff date (September 2021), including the United States, Canada, the United Kingdom,

Australia, France, Germany, Italy, Spain, and many others.

It is critical to note, however, that the provision of Google Play Books Partner Center may vary depending on a number of factors such as local laws and regulations, market demand, and Google's business strategies. Furthermore, the platform may not offer the identical set of tools and services in each country where it is available.

To discover see whether Google Play Books Partner Center is available in a particular country, visit the platform's official website or contact Google directly.

Publication on Partner Center

In order to publish your book on the partner center. The author's country must be in the list of countries offered by Google and an author must have a Gmail account.

In order to fully set up a Google partner account an author must provide the following details.

1. Legal Name.
2. Date of Birth.
3. Place of Residence.
4. Address.
5. Bank Information.
6. Tax Information.

Once all of the above information is fulfilled the Play Books Partner Center will be ready to publish the first book.

To publish the first book, go to the book catalog and follow the following steps.

1. Click "Add Book."
2. Select the selling options (Total of 3 different options are given, an author must select one of them according to his choice.)
3. Provide the ISBN or select Google book ID. The Google book ID is similar to Amazon's ASIN.

Book Information

In book information details an author has to provide all the necessary details of the book.

1. Book Title and Subtitle.
2. Book Description.
3. Book Language.
4. Release Date of the Book.
5. Book Audience.
6. Book Format
7. Page Count of Book.
8. Select the Book Genres.
9. Author Name and Biography

10. Add Book Series (if any).

11. Select Book Appearance in Google Search.

Book Contents

In book content details an author has to provide all the necessary details of the book.

1. Provide the manuscript of the book

2. Provide the eBook cover.

Book Pricing

In this section, an author has to select the effective pricing of his book. He can either select the currency either British Pounds, US dollars, or Euro.

Book Review

This is the final step. An author must review every detail that he has provided on the platform to ensure its correctness. Once every detail is ensured the author can click "publish" button to publish the book. The publication process may take a few days to pass the Google review. Once the review is passed the book will be live on Google and Google Play Books.

Rule # Sixteen

AUTHOR SOCIAL MEDIA PLATFORMS

Author social media platforms are essential for an author's success. Every celebrity, politician, and entrepreneurs are available on various social media platforms. These social media platforms are direct connections to various readers and people for an author. A good profile on these social media not only boosts sales of an author but it also allows an author to connect with readers and talk to them personally.

Author social media platforms are world wide web platforms via which authors may connect with readers, market their books, and interact with their audience. Among the most popular author social media platforms are:

1. Twitter: It is a microblogging network where authors may make brief updates, communicate with readers and other authors, and promote their work.

2. Facebook: It is a popular social media network that authors can use to create a book page or connect with fans and other authors.

3. Instagram: It is a photo-sharing app that authors can use to publish photographs relating to their books or writing process, connect with readers, and promote their work.

4. Goodreads: It is a social media platform dedicated to book lovers. Authors can build a profile and engage with readers while also sharing book suggestions and promoting their own work.

5. YouTube: It is a video-sharing network that authors may use to market their work by creating book trailers, author interviews, and other video content.

6. LinkedIn: It is a professional networking site where authors may connect with other writers, publishers, and literary agents.

These are just a handful of social media platforms that are used by most of the authors. The most reputable is Goodreads.

Goodreads is a reader and author social networking platform that allows people to discover, review, and share books with their friends and the larger online community. Otis Chandler and Elizabeth Khuri Chandler started it in December 2006, and Amazon purchased it in March 2013.

Goodreads is primarily a platform for readers to keep track of their reading progress, discover new books, and connect with other readers. People can organize their readings by creating virtual bookshelves, rating and reviewing books, and joining or creating reading groups. The platform also provides book recommendations based on the reader's reading history as well as the ratings and reviews of other users who have similar reading preferences.

One of the most significant advantages of Goodreads is its massive reader community. It's an excellent place to interact with other book readers and get new book recommendations, with over 100 million users. Users can follow authors and see what their friends are reading, in addition, to participating in book and author discussions with the other readers.

Goodreads has also evolved into a valuable tool for authors and publishers, as it enables them to network with readers and market their books. Authors can create profiles, engage with readers, provide freebies, and promote their books through advertising and other tools. Publishers may employ the site to launch new books, connect with readers, and 's importance for upcoming publications.

Goodreads, in additional to its social networking elements, provides a number of other important resources for readers. For example, the Goodreads Choice Awards allow readers to vote for their favourite books of the year in a variety of categories. The Reading Challenge tool enables users to create and track reading objectives, which gives them a sense of accomplishment and motivates them to read more.

Overall, Goodreads is a wonderful forum for all types of book enthusiasts. Whether you're a casual or a voracious reader, the platform provides a plethora of tools and community features that make reading more pleasant and social. It's a must-have for anyone who wants to find new books, interact with other readers, or promote their own work.

Rule # Seventeen

AUTHOR BIOGRAPHY

Author biography is really important for an author. A perfect author biography not only boosts sales but also brings ample opportunities for an author. It help author get interviews, promotion, call on events, and much more.

As a self-published author, the author's biography is an important part of the book's marketing strategy. When people pick up the book or go to the author's website, this is the first thing they see. A well-written author bio will help you establish the credentials as a writer and persuade people to learn more about your work.

Here are some ideas for writing an author biography as a self-published author:

1. Keep it short: The author bio should be no more than 250 words long. Stick to the most important details about yourself, such as the writing experience, education, and any awards received.

2. Display the author's writing style: An author bio is an opportunity for him to demonstrate his writing abilities. Write in a style that complements your book while also being easy to read and enjoyable.

3. Highlight the distinguishing characteristics: What distinguishes you from other writers? Do you have a distinct background or point of view that influences your writing? Make a point of emphasizing these attributes in your author profile.

4. Include a professional headshot: Including a professional headshot in the author bio provides a personal touch and allows readers to connect with the author.

5. Link to your website and social media: Include links to your website and social media profiles in your author bio. This allows readers to discover more about you and your work while also connecting with you.

6. Avoid exaggeration: While it may be tempting to inflate the accomplishments, it is critical to be truthful in the author bio. Avoid making false statements or inflating your experience by sticking to the facts.

7. Update the author bio on a frequent basis, especially if you publish new works or acquire fresh awards. Keep it up to date and relevant to your present writing profession.

Note that the author bio is an important part of the book's marketing strategy. Take the time to write a fascinating and succinct biography that highlights the writing style, distinguishing characteristics, and successes as a self-published author. One may establish a strong personal brand and attract new readers to the work by doing so.

Rule # Eighteen

AUTHOR WEBSITE

Author website is an important tool for becoming a well-noted author on the internet. An author's website is the direct connection between the readers and authors.

The website is one of the most significant marketing tools in the arsenal as an author. It's the web home, where readers can find out more about author, his works, and his writing process. A well-designed and regularly updated author website can assist in establishing the brand, connecting with readers, and effectively promoting the work.

Establishes the author brand: The website is a representation of an author brand. It helps readers to view the writing style, personality, and distinguishing characteristics. One can build a consistent image across all of the marketing channels by creating a website to reflect the brand.

Connects with readers: The website serves as a direct means of communicating with the readers. It provides a means to contact with the audience, share updates, and participate in debates. It may generate loyal followers who will buy the books and suggest the author to other readers.

Displays the work: A website is the ideal spot to display authors' books cover art, blurbs, and reviews. To attract readers to buy the book.

Provides useful information: The author's website can also act as a clearinghouse for information about the author's writing process, forthcoming events, and other news. The author can keep readers engaged and informed about his work by sharing this information.

Increases online visibility: A website can assist auththe or to increase online visibility. Author may rank better in search results and attract more readers to his work by optimizing his website for search engines.

Sells books: Author website can also serve as an effective sales tool. One can make it easy for readers to buy his work directly from his website by offering links to purchase his books.

In conclusion, having an author website is critical for developing your brand, communicating with readers, and effectively advertising your work. You may develop a strong online presence and attract new readers to your work by creating a well-designed and regularly updated website.

Sheikh Muhammad Ibraheem the author of this book provides excellent services in website development for indie authors. To get more information on web development contact the author at (https://sheikhibraheem.com)

Rule # Nineteen

BOOK MARKETING AND DISTRIBUTION

Book marketing and distribution are very essential for a self-published author. In traditional publication, the publication company is responsible for marketing and distribution of the book. In the case of the self-publication author is responsible for the marketing and distribution of the book.

The biggest problem is finding the right readers for the book. There are various distribution and marketing platforms that a self-published author can use.

There are various eBook distributors and aggregators that an author can use to promote and distribute his books worldwide.

Smashwords is a well-known eBook distribution site. If an author submits his book to them, it will be distributed through Apple Books, Barnes & Noble, Kobo, and a variety of additional retailers and library networks. They will provide an author with a free ISBN if author request one. They also provide an author with daily sales data from the top merchants, allowing them to track how well their book is performing.

This new aggregator website has a slick design and a modern feel to it. Draft2Digital's distribution network is not as extensive as Smashwords', but it includes all of the big players, including Kobo, Barnes & Noble, iBooks, and Amazon KDP. Furthermore, you get a sizable 60% royalty on sales. Its automated formatting services, which convert any text file into a professional, smart eBook, are the buzz of the town.

Publish Drive is a Hungary-based aggregator that assists writers in telling their stories as easily as possible. They provide authors and publishers with cutting-edge publishing tools and access to global and specialty markets. PublishDrive accepts a variety of payment methods. Subscribers have the option of either a monthly subscription plan or income sharing.

They were pioneers in the eBook aggregator industry in introducing a flat monthly cost. So, if you are an author who sells at least $1,000 each month, you can keep 100% of your royalties by paying a monthly charge of $100, regardless of the actual sales amount. Publish Drive debuted eBook, audio, and print distribution in March 2020 in an effort to make their platform more user-friendly, making them the only aggregators to handle all three formats for thousands of book outlets.

Streetlib was released in 2006. "Our strength is in our team," their business motto says. They are headquartered in Italy and have operations in Europe, Africa, and North America. They have offices in New York as well as India. Among their competitors, they have the strongest global footprint. They strive to help local and international authors flourish in the dynamic digital publishing ecosystem by providing all available assistance. Streetlib treats each account individually and gives superior analytics. To get started, simply establish an account with your billing information and upload your books. The aggregator earns a distribution commission on actual sales, ensuring that all parties benefit.

Ingram Spark is a major distributor of paperback and eBooks. Ingram Spark is a possibility if you want a single aggregator that can distribute paperbacks, hardcovers, and eBooks. They cover the majority of shops.

Lulu is one of the earliest paperback distributors. They also allow you to distribute your eBooks. It's choice for authors who wish to utilize a single aggregator for both paperbacks and eBooks.

The eBook industry is one of the largest industries in the book market. For an author, it is a struggle of years and good business strategies to become a successful author in the world. A successful self-published author is self-motivated, has no fear, and is willing to devote as much time as he possibly can.

THE END

75